RAISE
THE
DEAD!

RAISE THE DEAD!

MYRON C. MADDEN

WORD BOOKS
PUBLISHER
WACO, TEXAS

First Paperback Printing: April 1979

RAISE THE DEAD!
Copyright © 1975 by Word, Incorporated

Library of Congress catalog card number: 74–27483
Printed in the United States of America

Scripture quotations marked RSV are from the Revised
Standard Version of the Bible, copyrighted 1946 (renewed
1973), 1956 and © 1971 by the Division of Christian
Education of the National Council of the Churches of Christ
in the U.S.A. and used by permission.

To

Mary Ben,

whose touch has a special life-giving quality

Contents

Part II

Toward a Method and Reason in Healing from Death

Introduction

In 1955 Paul Tillich delivered the graduation address at Union Theological Seminary on the subject "Heal the sick; cast out the demons." He took his text from Matthew 10:8 where Jesus said to his disciples, "Heal the sick, raise the dead, cleanse lepers, cast out demons" (RSV). While Tillich delivered a masterful address, I wondered why he left out the hard part of the command—"raise the dead." These pages attempt to deal with what Jesus might have meant by such a strange order. Surely he did not literally mean for the disciples to wake up dead people.

Because Jesus spoke in the symbol and sign of parables, it is not always easy to know what he actually meant. For example, in his "inaugural speech" at Nazareth, Jesus quoted Isaiah as part of his own mission, saying the Lord had anointed him for "recovering of sight to the blind" (Luke 4:18, RSV). Yet there are actually few cases reported where the blind recovered their sight. Rather blindness is the inability to see the more obvious realities in the human pilgrimage. Jesus referred to the Pharisees as "blind guides" (Matt. 15:14, RSV).

If Jesus was talking about something else when he mentioned blindness, then it is possible that his reference to raising the dead meant something other than a literal restoration of vital function to dead persons. The New Testament record tells of Jesus restoring life in a very limited number of cases. It was reported that Jairus's daughter was dead, but Jesus said she was only sleeping. In any event she was healed or raised (Mark 5:35–42). Then we have the story of Lazarus being raised; only John's Gospel gives the account (John 11:11–44).

On the basis of Scripture accounts, the focus of Jesus' work was not on raising the dead. He gives emphasis to a new birth—the necessity of dying to one thing and coming alive to another. In the story of the Prodigal Son (Luke 15:11–24) the father justifies the celebration on the son's homecoming saying, "For this my son was dead, and is alive again" (11:24, RSV). The Apostle Paul also spoke frequently of being "dead to sin," "dead to the law," etc., and of "walking in newness of life."

I am not setting aside the importance of the Apostolic interpretations of the Christ event; however, I want to explore what the words "raise the dead" mean to me and the persons I know as we attempt to encounter death meaningfully. So many people have death in them and need to get it out. They need the freedom and vitality that comes in not having to wear death as an albatross about their necks.

Through many years of counseling experience I have observed how frequently death becomes a crippling agent in the lives of persons, and I have been privileged in some of those encounters to help remove the curse, the sting, and the power of death from living people. It is my hope to share here whatever constructive knowledge I have gained: to help every reader to "raise his own dead." Thus I am bold to propose a new type of therapy, one which is meant to release us to all kinds of creativity and meaning. The emphasis is threefold:

1. Getting Life Out of Death

Childhood fears and terrors connected with death tend to retain the same strong impact as do childhood associations with ether and spinach. We need to clean them out, update, and correct them —to cancel out the false psychology that ascribes mobility or an unreal vitality to death.

2. Getting Death Out of Life

The actual loss of a loved one often encases death inside us because we hold on to the loved one in unreal ways. When we identify with the dead in such a way as to take the place of the dead, we begin to die ourselves. To "raise the dead" here means finding a way to let the dead be dead, in a final and clean way.

3. Dealing with the Death of a Relationship

It is almost impossible to live without losing a relationship now and then. Occasionally we lose a most important one and are unable to do much about it, except to deny its defeat, or prolong its agony in fantasy. We need the courage to let dead relationships die, giving us the freedom to get out of the past and to live in a more creative way in the present.

Part II of this book deals both with specific problems in applying the therapy proposed in the first three chapters and the philosophy on which the therapy is based. Further application of the therapy as occasioned by the current widespread concern with demonology, witchcraft, and exorcism is the subject of the final chapter.

PART I

Raise the Dead:
A Proposal for a New Therapy

1.
Getting Life Out of Death

The Childhood Fears and Terrors

Repression as a death force

The preschool child repeats the whole history of the human race in a six-year span. He goes through nearly all human emotions ranging from joy to sorrow, terror to delight. Sigmund Freud was the master pioneer who made modern man aware of the importance of these early years in the shaping and influencing of life style.

Freud taught that most of the troubles we encounter in adult life stem from the many prohibitions that are laid on us as small children. He tended to narrow the troubles (the neuroses) down to the handling and mishandling of the sex drive, primarily the repression of the sex drive in one way or another: "I must repeat . . . that these psychoneuroses, as far as my experience goes, are based on the motive power of the sexual instinct. I do not mean that the energy of the sexual instinct merely contributes to the forces supporting the morbid manifestations (symptoms), but I advisedly maintain that this contribution supplies the only constant and most important source of energy in the neuroses."[1]

Freud taught us all about the mechanism of *repression*, of how we are able to bury unacceptable data for a generation without any of it coming to awareness, except indirectly through dream, daydream, and fantasy. He developed a fine art of tracing down the signals so that as a psychoanalyst he could follow this all back to childhood in his patients.

Though I owe a heavy debt to Freud, I want to call attention to an important area he overlooked or neglected: the area of the *prohibition*—the *threat of death*—that we adults communicate to children in one way or another to control their impulses.

A young woman of twenty-one whom I was counseling suddenly remembered some innocent sex play

---

[1] *The Sexual Aberrations in the Basic Writings of Sigmund Freud*, tr. A. A. Brill (New York: Random House, 1938), p. 573.

with her older brothers when she must have been about five years of age. Telling me about it, she grew tense, anxious and frightened. She said her brothers had threatened to kill her if she ever told it. By the time she finished the story, she was able to see how harmless the whole thing was. But the damage had persisted because she had believed all this time that she had been witness to something that would cause her death. Although she said she had not remembered the event in the sixteen years between, needless to say, it troubled and tortured her. It erupted into awareness when the warmth of the counseling relationship helped the forbidden data to come to the surface. Even so, she confessed that her feelings told her I would probably take a chair and execute the expected judgment by killing her.

The case of this young woman was certainly one of sexual repression, but my argument is simply this: *what we repress is not as significant as the power we use to repress.* Through repression we can implant a horrible fear of destruction in a child.

The child and time

Usually in the fourth to fifth year a child learns about time—about before and after. Right away he asks two questions: where did I come from and where am I going. In searching out the first question he learns, in one way or another, about sex as his origin. His discovery can be painful, shameful, disgusting, frightening. But it is also exciting, warming, and enticing. As he identifies with those who brought him into being he finds it is not all bad. But time has two ends and he probes in the direction of his destiny, of where he is going. He gets the answer in the death of a pet, or in the death of a person. This discovery is shocking, bewildering, and full of horror. It has no good in it and no ability to excite except in a dreadful manner. He can handle the data around birth and sex, but he can't handle the experience which lets him know that he is marked for decay and extinction.

Freud was right that the sexual instincts were the material most often repressed by children. These impulses are met with such strong prohibition that children feel they absolutely have to put them under wrappers. But that prohibition—"Forget it on pain of death"—is the key to many neuroses that crop out later in life.

Take the young woman again: she had a problem of sexual frigidity. Doesn't the word *frigid* imply coldness? If she questioned her origin in sex, she would be squeezed by her destiny in death: a mixing of the ends. Death is cold, sex is warm. When you mix sex and death by using death threat to control impulse, you are using the cold stuff to hold down the hot stuff. The icy layer of death fear can complicate the feelings until, in the end, the assumption is that there can be no sex unless there is a death. Eric

Berne says a girl "may even get the idea that she will die if she has an orgasm."[2] When the fear of death gets mixed with the desire for sexual expression, it makes women frigid and men impotent. The dead need to be raised! Before we get into the "how" of answering this need, let us look at the potency of the prohibition that locks the feelings in and perverts the flow of vitality.

Shades of witchcraft

To put it mildly, little children are constantly in motion and in action; they probe, test, examine, inquire, search, ask, and meddle. All this is to the exasperation of parents, especially if they have several small children at one time. So parents are constantly on guard to protect the child from a thousand ways he might harm himself. And though the child usually wants to please his parents, he constantly tests the limits of his space and his permission. He is repeatedly running into prohibitions while the exasperated parents tend to use any prohibition that will work to restrain the galloping impulses. The child will usually stop where he is met with pain (earlier) and fear (later).

In a few short years the child experiences first-hand, at the feeling level, many of the various pro-

---

[2] Eric Berne, M.D., *What Do You Say After You Say Hello?* (New York: Bantam Books, 1973), p. 49.

hibitions that historically have been used to keep
unacceptable impulses from running rampant: witchcraft, taboo, magic, divination, sorcery, and the like.
All these approaches are more or less aimed at control
through fear, the fear that is generated by fear of
death—or perhaps we should say a *fear of the dead*.

There is a world of difference at the feeling level
in being afraid of death in general and in being afraid
of a particular dead person who is supposed to have
some kind of power to work harm and evil to you.
The defenses against such fear get pretty weak after
nightfall, especially where the imagination populates
every dark corner with phantom apparitions. Just as
the wish can create the mirage of fulfillment, so fear
in a negative way can conjure up what is dreaded.
"The thief fears every bush an officer," says Shakespeare, and again, "Present fears are less than horrible
imaginings."

Scientifically speaking, death really has no power.
But a child does not always learn about death scientifically. Rather he may learn about it emotionally
through ghost stories or horror movies seen on television.

Such a psychology of death denies the biology of
death. Biology teaches that *life* is on the aggressive
march. If you throw a dead rat into the swamp, life
moves in on it and competes viciously for every par-
ticle of this bonus that has been dropped.

The concept of death that a child learns early is
one that is akin to that held by the devotees of witch-

craft in the West Indies. When the child sees that death, instead of being still, silent and motionless, is animated and activated so that it becomes ambulatory and predatory, he learns a reverse psychology akin to witchcraft, in which death is imagined to have the power to kill whatever it touches. The idea is reinforced when the child observes how adults *feel* about death. He notices that they don't touch it; they stand in some kind of abhorrence of it. They come apart at funerals and generally reveal completely unrealistic attitudes about something that is altogether natural.

Further complications arise when religion is brought into the picture to allay the fears of the child, to say that the dead person is in the care of God or that death is what God wanted for him. We affirm that Jesus takes these relatives away and "takes care of them." God and Jesus are often imaged to be in the death business, a sort of cosmic version of the funeral director. So whatever they touch comes under the spell, and "come to God" may arouse the same feelings as "go to God." When God touches you, the same thing happens that happened to grandpa when he died. Is it any wonder that children "fear" God? They just don't have the ability to get God out of the death category at an early age, especially in view of the fact that we usually associate God with death more than any other one experience in the mind of childhood.

Thus religion, instead of putting things right for

the child, instead of becoming a comfort and a support, may get contaminated with all things associated with death. It may take a few years before the child is able to update his feelings so he can accept meaningful religious support.

All of this is really to say that *death has no power*. The strength of witchcraft comes from investing enormous energies into the region of the dead in order to bring about impulse control according to the wishes of the ones practicing witchcraft.

We don't practice witchcraft on our children knowingly, but wherever we allow death to become active, we develop a distorted psychology of death and we deny the biology of death. We ignore the fact that life is aggressively absorbing all death, and we forget that death has no power over life. We then cause our children to split the energies of life so that a dread-full amount of the available energy is invested in death. Death then rises up to control life, to chill it, to distort it, to pervert it. And it can only act with the energy we invest from ourselves.

The neuroses of life infest those areas where we deny the realities and establish false beliefs in their place. We become neurotic more by the nature of the deathlike prohibition than by the vital material we drive under the surface through repression. What we repress *with* becomes more important than *what* we repress. For example, it is not the fear of sex with which we repress sex, but with the fear of death or some implied threat. It is important to realize that children don't always have to be threatened with ultimates in order to *feel* an ultimate. For example, the words "I won't love you if you do that" carry with them in the child's imagination a chain of associations that may go something like this: "If she doesn't love me she might leave me; she might not feed me and take care of me; she might give me away; she might forget me and leave me all alone . . . and I might die." I'm not saying parents tell children they will be murdered if they lose control; the message gets through in indirect ways—communicated through the feelings. We can't repress with anything stronger than the fear of death because there is nothing stronger. In fact the fear of death is the energy that controls impulse, and that fear is unreal. The child will not be killed; yet after repeated threats that bring up the fear of death, the child may even finally decide he can take a few risks and probe the limits just to see how far he can go before the sentence is passed.

Here in early childhood we begin to build the denial process around death, it being too painful to handle otherwise. And when we have reached the point where we can deny life's great reality, death, then it becomes relatively easy to deny lesser realities. We need to give the adult a chance to get the witchcraft-like horror out of the spirit of his child-of-the-past. We need to raise the dead! But death can't be raised or removed or made acceptable and understandable unless it is faced as a reality; not in its horror-ridden imagined reality as a power-on-the-march but as a friendly factor in our human pilgrimage and a necessary part of it.

Getting the good dream

When he was five, one of my children was plagued with nightmares after his grandmother died. In the middle of the night he aroused me with a pitiful plea: "Daddy, can you help me get a good dream?" I knew what was troubling him and I knew that the only thing I could do was to love him and assure him that I loved him. This was enough to drive away his death fears in the night, and he went back to sleep.

As adults we very often have the same need to get rid of the childhood images of terror. And we can't do that until we get a good dream.

I talked with a woman who was still suffering from the death of her mother six months after the loss. When she wept, her face took on the image of death; her lips came back, exposing her teeth in a cadaverous grimace: a sign to me that she was still tied up in her identification with her mother. She said the loss of her mother had made her feel that "all the warmth had gone out of the world," and she could not get rid of that feeling. Finally she began to work through her grief as she wept all the way down into her pain, still showing the image of death on her countenance. Emotionally she was looking on death through the childhood fears. In the process of working back through them, she had a dream that brought her a beautiful memory of her mother. It gradually over-powered all the feelings of coldness and separation and was reinforced when she found a picture of her mother in which she looked much the same as she had in the dream. The dream and the picture together formed a solid basis on which she could feel blessed-ness and warmth. In effect they restored her to man-ageable function, allowing her to cope with a host of problems that otherwise might have been too much for her. We can't underestimate the strength of the "good dream" as a way of overcoming powerful childhood dread. This is a vital part of raising the dead.

Most of us have many good memories that may have gotten lost under stress and crisis. With the cold of winter upon us, we sometimes forget the beauty and warmth of spring. At such times the touch of a friend can often help us see that the curve down the road is not the end of the road. The other person can help us hold on in trust and patience, and the warmth of another can help some good memories come to the surface.

Childhood fears in adult grief

The person who lost a loved one in early child-hood will frequently have special difficulty dealing with adult grief. One woman whom I asked if she had been able to give up her father remarked, "I never really got to my father's funeral. I was stuck back on my little sister's funeral that came when I was six." She went on to relate how completely her sister's death had shattered her parents, so that in this funeral for her father, she felt mainly the dread that everyone was going to fall to pieces as they had done before. Before she could fully deal with the loss of her father it was necessary for her to deal with the earlier funeral of her sister.

It is important to realize that death and grief are not the same thing. A child may learn about death as fact by observing or experiencing it at reasonable distance in his emotions; or he may learn about it through the loss of someone very dear and close.

When the first deep awareness of death and loss comes about as a neighbor dies or someone not closely related, the child has a chance to deal with death in a little more realistic way. He can put himself into the picture without having to deal with grief along with death. The child who can learn about death in this way is fortunate indeed. Death teaches the child that he is mortal, and that's enough for him to attempt to digest at one time.

But if the child learns about death in a grief experience, he may get the processes mixed up. Grief— the pain over losing someone or something that the child is invested in—makes the child feel something

has been taken away *from* him; death makes him fear
something is going to be done *to* him.

Sometimes a child has to learn that he is mortal and
that he must give up someone dear all in one big crisis. In the case described at the beginning of this sec-
tion, the stigma and pain of the funeral for the little
sister had hovered over all loss or possible loss for a
generation. Hence death was so charged with the
ability to crush and devastate relatives that the child-
inside-the-woman was determined to have no more
funerals in her family forever. There was no way,
then, for her to have a funeral without going back to
the first one, in the same way an adult returns to the
sickening smell of ether many years after a childhood
operation.

Adults just have a bigger problem accepting grief
or dealing with grief if they had a painful or horrify-
ing childhood experience with it. A man of twenty-
eight, remembering the scene of his grandmother's
funeral some twenty-three years before, avoided his
grandfather's funeral. His mother had struggled and
fought with him then to get him to "kiss grandmother good-by" which he stubbornly refused to
do. Now he feared the same scene to be repeated
even though his mother was a small woman and he
was a rather large man. His feelings still brought
forth a dread of a repeat of what happened so long
before.

Get life out of death

It is very important that we learn not to give so much power to the "kiss of death"; that is, that we not allow death to kill us wherever it touches us. Death does not move, it does not stir, it does not talk, it cannot act except in the imagination. If we give it the power, our own strength, then it can destroy us.

If we cling to the dead, we invest them with some imaginary form of existence: positive or negative. If we are loving persons, we tend to hold to the dead to get them to bless us in some way. If we are more suspicious and fearful, we allow the dead to persecute us and haunt us. While we get frightened as children by the ghost stories we hear or the TV pictures we see, it is important that we allow science to be of service to us. Science takes no stock in communicating with the dead nor in frightening living people with some kind of movable death image. Our own need to talk to the dead can make the imagination produce the dead for our perverted or unreal purposes.

Signs of life in death

By speaking of signs of life in death I do not mean some physical characteristic such as *rigor mortis*, but rather manifestations of a kind of psychology (often a carryover from childhood) where the kiss of death has the ability to kill. Adults make all kinds of such unreal responses in dealing with death. Listed below are just a few of these "signs of life in death":

» A person goes to great length to avoid funerals.

» A person becomes a compulsive attender of funerals. (One woman I know was upset with one of the two funeral homes in her town because funerals were scheduled simultaneously and she couldn't make both of them. She didn't know either of the deceased persons, but she felt compelled to go to all funerals.)

» A person has such fear of touching a corpse that it drives him to panic.

» A person feels a compulsion to touch the dead when it is not necessary or appropriate to do so.

» A person chooses a work that will constantly put him in contact with dying people. (Of course this is not always the case; many people who have worked through their hang-ups at this point render great service both in medicine and nursing.)

» A minister finds himself unable to conduct a funeral service. (This *could* be his past unresolved data pouring to the surface so that he fears losing control of his feelings.)

» The doctor finds that he is unable to deliver the "word" to the family. (This *could* be a sign that he can't accept the truth for himself.)

» A person surrounds himself with macabre, ghostly pictures.

» A person takes unusual delight in frightening others with stories and pictures of death.

» A person spends his leisure reading or writing stories centering on the grotesque (e.g., Edgar Allan Poe's *The Pit and the Pendulum* or François Mauriac's *The Kiss to the Leper*).

» A person has an obsessive fear of a cemetery at night.

The list could go on endlessly and I will leave it to the reader to supply his own data, which may need updating from the shadowy regions of the early years.

Cast out demons

The medieval notion that the ghosts disappeared at daybreak has some truth in it. The light of day tends to clear up the frightful images of the night. The adult has a right to allow the light of reason to shine into the dark corners of past fears. But when past fears have the ability to drive us to panic, we are still investing death with powers it doesn't really possess.

Some of our "demons" get their existence from our imagination and need to be cast out; we need to be free from living among the tombs as was the Gerasene demoniac whom Jesus liberated from the legion of evil spirits (Mark 5:1–17). As I see it, Jesus freed him from the death stuff he must have been carrying when he could shift his existence from the graveyard to the community. This change must have been accomplished both with the light of reason and the warmth of a loving acceptance.

Most of us know how hard it is to reason away our fears; many of them got inside us before we could reason much. Even when we learn what the fears are, why they got there and how they hold to us, they may still fail to go away. At this point we need the courage to quit feeding these monsters no matter how strongly we are convinced that their death will make us feel our own death. Persons who know what it is to allow their own monsters to die of starvation can be of much help here, for our great fears are not mastered by intelligence so much as by the courage to walk through them.

A man whose mother died when he was eight carried a childhood resolve never to have another woman die on him. When he married, his wife controlled him by getting sick. He has no chance for living freely and fully unless he can somehow take the risk that her illness at any given time *could* result in her death. If he can't let her get sick and if he can't stand the thought of losing her, he can't live and he can't let her have any freedom to live. The freedom to die is a part of the freedom to live.

Our fears reach monstrous and demonic proportions when we are scared to death of death, but when the fear of death loses its grip, the monsters within us have no strength.

Beyond Fear

Our source of dread and uncommon fear is nearly always the child within us. Seldom does it come from adult experience. The child, unable to cope with the emotions arising from encounters with his possible destruction, represses them. From then on, even into adulthood, they are available to drag him right back through unreasonable fears. Here are some guidelines for helping get beyond the childhood data:

» Accept the fact that nearly every adult has some unreasonable fear.

» Realize that it is a comfort to other people when you can share some of your own unreasonable fear with them. It comforts them to know that they are not the only ones having these things. Ask someone to share your fears rather than go through them alone. The Apostles went *out* two by two; we should go *in* two by two.

» Be prepared for the fact that although what you fear seems great, it may be almost a nothing. The problem comes in the wrapping of the package, not in its contents. Our imagination loads the package with fissionable material or lethal explosives, but usually it contains only some harmless substance.

» Be prepared for the letdown when you find yourself spending so much emotion on fear of a trivial or small thing.

» Don't force yourself into an artificial situation to get the fear out. Let it come up in the normal routine and stress of life.

» Try not to keep avoiding the pain of the fear. If it is there, face it with the help of a friend who understands and accepts. Your fears don't frighten your friend; he has fears from his own childhood, which are probably all different in the particulars.

» Be willing to accept professional help if you honestly feel the need.

» Do what you must to accept your own mortality. Allow birthdays, anniversaries, New Year's Day observances, or even the mirror to speak to you. People can accept their age without being morbid and morose; they can celebrate their life when they accept the life that is theirs.

» Let the biology of death correct the childish psychology of death. Biology says life is the aggressive, thrusting, pulsating force, and it takes any death as a bonus. Death has no power but the power we give it. Be prepared to let death be stripped of all its horror. When that happens, death takes its rightful place as a friend of man and nature. When we destroy the capital city of death, the kingdom of fear begins to fall.

2.
Getting Death Out of Life

The Place of and Need for Grief

It is very difficult to accept the absolute physical separation death brings from the person or thing taken. It is so difficult, in fact, that we may refuse to acknowledge the separation and attempt to keep the dead with us in some way.

When we bypass or ignore the grief that normally follows the death of a loved one we run a grave risk. Because grief is a process through which we are able to separate or draw a line between life and death, it helps us remove death from our lives. It is a very natural process that helps us separate from the person in whom we have invested a part of our lives.

The death of a loved one is the line of separation. We cannot cross that barrier and we are not called on to do so. Rather we come to a mourning that helps us surrender what we have invested of ourselves into the person we have lost. When we insist on "keeping faith" with the dead by not accepting their death, we deprive ourselves of the very process which restores our loss so that our life can be reinvested. We need to realize that grief is our friend to help us deal with the hurt over the loss of a loved one. And we need also to realize that since we grow gradually into a relationship with a person, we are unable suddenly to take it all back. Grief time is the time of giving our feelings a chance to catch up with what our minds know immediately when death occurs.

We may go round and round the same track in the imagination, repeatedly going over and over the history that leads up to the shock until we wear the ruts smooth. But we keep on coming back to the hard, cold fact of separation until at last our feelings absorb the truth.

Tears and crying are a useful part of the grief process too, helping the emotions to purge themselves and to come to terms with the reality that must be faced. Some people do their mourning without tears, but most people find that crying helps.

Most important, grief is our way of getting our life back from the one who has died. Life cannot remain with the dead: where we try to make this happen death and life get mixed in a strange way so that the living person comes to absorb the dead person. In this attempt to hold onto the dead, the living person will need to be raised from his own dying.

It is a very common thing for us to express every wish that we could have died in the place of our loved one; and we think of the ways this might have been possible, but really get nowhere. We don't actually have that kind of choice open to us no matter how much we wish it.

Stages in Grief[1]

If grief could come as a steadily mounting thing, most of us could probably manage better. But it seems to come in snatches, in sudden bursts of awareness, and just as quickly closes up again. The stages in grief tend to go something like the following:

Impossible. This is the original resistance to acceptance of the mortality of someone we love. This just can't be; we don't want to face it; we deny that it ever can be.

Possible. This is where the word of the doctor gets through to us that our loved one doesn't have much chance of pulling through. We contemplate the seriousness of the medical situation and we vow to do all we can to stave off the unwanted result. We ponder

[1] For a very competent study and elaboration of the stages of grief, see *On Death and Dying* by Elisabeth Kübler-Ross, M.D. (New York: Macmillan, 1970).

our own inadequacies, failures, blunders, and acts of unkindness. We feel guilty.

Impending. In this stage we begin to come to terms with what is happening. The suffering our loved one is experiencing brings our feelings to greater acceptance of death. Here we get into all kinds of trouble. We feel that death would stop the suffering. It would solve financial problems; it would solve personal expenditures of energy, long nights of wondering and slow days of waiting. More guilt builds up. We come to realize that death might solve as many problems as it would create, and we don't like to think that.

We want to measure our grief properly because if we give the person up to death before death, we would be too hasty with our grief. If we hold it back too much, we feel inappropriate. We don't know how much grief to express and how much to hold back. We are also perplexed about where to express our grief—in front of our loved one, or in the corridor?

Then we don't know how to manage our eyes. We want them to reflect hope when they feel despair or hopelessness. Though we want to keep courage high in the sick person while we are running low, our eyes may give this away.

Fact. When death occurs, most people take the fact. But often, the happening makes the relative or friend have to go back through the stages just mentioned. When death becomes fact, we may still have some feeling about its impossibility in spite of having gone through that stage and in a way accepted the possibility. Nevertheless the experiences leading up to death help prepare persons for the event of death in the way that practice helps with the real game of football.

And in most cases where all the preparatory stages have been practiced, they do prove helpful in meeting the actual test of the death event.

Shock. When the message of loss reaches the feelings they go into shock. It is as if the living were suddenly invaded with death. When a person loses the ability to feel, he is actually in a semi-death state. The message of death has brought some of the feelings of death to those deeply involved in loss.

The shock serves a good purpose in allowing the necessary time to prepare for the funeral and take care of other details. It also allows a person to feel something of death, thus relieving the bereaved of the need to die for the deceased. In a small way the shock is a kind of death.

During the time of shock the world of nature and society seem out of joint. Food tastes like chips and sawdust, flowers look like weeds, and a sunset looks like the insides of a churning stomach.

Shakespeare has the grieving Hamlet speak:

> O, that this too, too solid flesh would melt,
> Thaw and resolve itself into a dew!

Or that the Everlasting had not fix'd
His canon 'gainst self-slaughter! O God! God!
How weary, stale, flat, and unprofitable
Seem to me all the uses of this world!
                              (*Hamlet*, I, ii)

Hamlet continues:

I have of late . . . lost all my mirth, foregone all
custom of exercises; and indeed it goes so heavily
with my disposition that this goodly frame, the
earth, seems to me a sterile promontory . . .
                              (II, ii)

It is customary procedure with many doctors to
give a sedative of some sort to induce calm a little
ahead of the natural anesthesia. Sometimes this is as
much to protect the other patients in the hospital
setting as anything. Occasionally it protects the professional staff from their own sense of failure and
loss, and prevents their own unresolved griefs, if they
have them, from breaking through.

The shock may last hours or days, depending on
the circumstances and the personality of the one in
grief.

Post-Shock Awareness. During this period, the fact
of death comes through at a deeper level; the feelings have begun to take on the reality. There are oc-
casional bursts of deeper awareness, and these need to
be encouraged.

When the grief is doing its work, the wake and
the funeral serve as occasions to internalize what is
going on. It helps greatly if one can *see* and *touch*
the dead. The feelings are so set against accepting the
reality of death that they are helped if they have at
least two "witnesses"—the eye and the hand. Though
I would not force the one in grief to touch, I feel it
is good to provide the occasion for him to feel it's
okay to touch. We need to respect the childhood
terror that some people carry regarding an earlier experience of touching a dead relative.

Emotions in Grief

Grief stirs most of the emotions in one way or another. The order may vary from person to person,
but significant feelings come up to be managed. Supporting persons do well to let a person have a right
to whatever feelings are there.

Hostility. A six-year-old girl wouldn't put her
flowers on the casket of her father as the other mem-
bers of the family had done; she was expressing her
resentment at his dying. Shakespeare has Cleopatra
rage out in her loss of Antony:

> Hast thou no care of me? shall I abide
> In this dull world, which in thy absence is
> No better than a sty?
> . . . .
>   It were for me
> To throw my sceptre at the injurious gods,

> To tell them that this world did equal theirs
> Till they had stol'n our jewel.   (IV, xv)

Cleopatra expresses her anger at the dead Antony and at the very heavens for taking him. This is the way anger works if it can be expressed.

Supporting persons sometimes get frightened at this initial outburst of rage, but they need to know it is the right thing, if it is the felt thing. The hostility is natural because death is so terribly frustrating, nearly always provoking some anger feelings, whether or not they are verbalized.

Guilt. Death is failure in the feelings. Death to a loved one means that he has failed, while I have succeeded. There's no way to escape guilt when someone you love dies. I felt it terribly when my brother was killed on the battlefield—why did he have to die, leaving me the success of being alive? That same guilt was thunderous when I watched half the men in my outfit get killed or wounded in a single day. What right had I to be walking around? Why couldn't one of those sweet German shell bursts come along now and relieve me of all this guilt? I felt it even more strongly as I looked on my father in the casket. This was the strong, towering, powerful man to whom I looked as a child, saying I could never grow up and equal his strength. I took a childhood vow never to be his match, and now I stood over his prostrate, helpless form with my vows all broken.

There is the guilt of our secrets kept from our loved ones, of how we failed them, often made them unhappy, and put scars on their flesh. Now it's all too late. We can't put things right between us; we can't tell them we're sorry; we can't even get a chance to show them we wouldn't do it again.

Depression. This emotion may swamp us with self-accusation and a feeling that we have lost the ability to create, to be happy again, to dwell among the living by sharing ourselves with others. We get the feeling that what we give is worthless, what we do is useless, what we think is futile.

Despair. Basically this is a kind of emptiness. Expressed physically, it may even be a breathlessness. It is the feeling that vitality and life are just beyond our grasp. A very natural part of grief, it reflects the vacuum created by having a loved one torn by the roots from our own being. We despair that we are unable to fill up the empty place.

Helping with Grief

Much well-meaning help extended to grieving persons may not help them at all. We don't help much if we deny them their right to their feelings and their words, no matter what they say or do. We don't help with religion if we get resurrection in the picture too early. We don't help with assuring them God makes no mistakes, or saying this is all in the plan and will of God.

Help comes in accepting feelings, and especially in

giving the warm personal support that allows the other to weep to the depths of his being, even when his tears threaten to break things loose inside us.

The old Jewish idea of professional mourners was not a bad one. They were there to make enough mournful noise to protect the violent outpourings of the one in grief. We don't have many places where we can cry—out loud!

About the only place I have found is the automobile, while driving at night and with the windows rolled up. Our walls are too thin, our offices too crowded to provide the insulation that will allow a kind of "primal scream"—a really necessary outlet for our relief. This is the way we can break up the deep attachment to parents, mates or children, and this needs to be done for grief to run its course.

The helper needs to know that a person in grief will attempt to put off dealing with the deeper part of the grief. We might need to ask if he has dealt with the core of the pain, if he has walked into the very middle of his hurt. Give him no options for walking around the edge of the grief, nor of putting it off till a convenient time. The most appropriate time is the time nearest the death, the wake and the funeral and the days shortly following these.

The helper must avoid trying to fill the vacuum and take the place of the loss by being himself a sweet consolation. He can of course get the tears stopped and help the grieving person to return to function.

But when this happens, the healing will very probably be only temporary, with the core of the infection remaining to be dealt with at some later time.

What happens to people when they delay the solution of their grief? This becomes one of the truly needful situations where death enters life and needs to be gotten out: the dead need to be raised.

Delayed Grief

A case history

In January a pastor referred a lady of fifty-one to me for counseling who had lost her youngest daughter in an auto accident. Five college youths had also been killed in the same accident the previous August. She had not been able to accept the loss. She was depressed, fearful and anxious; she couldn't sleep without horrible dreams and her appetite was very poor. She was seeing a doctor to get sufficient medication to sleep a little and function in a limited way with her housework.

It was obvious that she was still going round in a daze; she was in mild shock and living mostly in fantasy. The burden of her fantasy kept repeating the conditions of the accident. When I asked if she was trying to get Marilyn back, she was startled, but she admitted that this was her wish, her dream and her hope. I further startled her by "permitting" her to have her wish, saying, "I want you to have Marilyn back. Go ahead and have it like you want it." She sat for some five minutes thinking, then remarked, "You can't have that. You can't get just your own child back; what about the other four? You'd have to get them all back if you got one back." To that I responded, "Then have them all back." She then launched into a lecture telling me how stupid my idea was. Then she pursued it further, "If you got her back, would she have to die again?" I answered, "I'll let you be the judge of that." She said, "Of course she would have to die again. You can't live forever on the earth. But that wouldn't be right for anybody to have to die twice. Once is enough." Then she went on to tell me something that happened "after Marilyn died." She caught herself. "I said Marilyn died; I've never said that before."

She was on her way. She had been dealing with her daughter's death as an impossibility, but now it was fact, and she was able to weep.

She tried to get her husband in for some help because he had completely avoided his own grief and was having some medical problems. By March she was showing increasing signs of being able to go on with her life; her husband entered the hospital for surgery.

There were many other details in the above case, but what I have related is an illustration of how often people seek solutions to grief that would only create greater problems if they got the solution they sought. Hence it was my approach simply to allow and encourage her to trace this solution out to the end. In so doing she realized that in trying to protect herself from the flood of grief, she had built her levee on the wrong side of the water. But she had to discover that for herself. When she did, she was able to come back toward reality where the suffering was, and where healing could be found.

I can't pass judgment on her husband medically, but his case illustrates many situations where in unresolved grief, physical stress becomes magnified. Our systems tend to show the stress about six months past the point of loss, give or take a few months.

The problems of holding on

It is strange, but true, that where people hold on to the dead, they begin to die. Whether this holding on is done out of love, faithfulness, or sometimes guilt, it takes the form of identifying with the dead. We can't identify with the dead without becoming like them. But if we lose a person who was wise and generous, and we identify with him in death, the significant feature about him now is not his wisdom and generosity, but his death.

I saw a young woman who almost lost two fingers from each hand because her hands had lost circulation. She was scheduled for surgery when in desperation she called in a psychiatrist. He spotted the case as one of unresolved grief. The woman had lost her father, who had never blessed her and loved her. She was literally holding to him for his blessing. The psychiatrist was able to help her work through the grief and her hands were restored to normal. When she repeated her story, her hands got cold and turned blue. The only way she could get death out of her was in giving up her father.

The mental dimension

A man of twenty-five, an only child, was told by his ailing father that he would have to be the brain of the family. The father died, leaving the son the task of running a business and taking care of his alcoholic mother. The son took the father's place almost too soon to complete his grief. We don't grieve when we take the place of the dead: at the primitive level of feelings the empty place is filled, so why grieve? Eight years later when I saw the son I discovered he had never grieved for his father. His chief symptom was one of amnesia: he had become the "brain" of the family and business, but the brain was functioning poorly. I sent him back to the cemetery where he had never visited. It was there he began to grieve for his father and finally give him up. As he accomplished this his brain was cleared of the amnesia and began to be aware of everything going on around him; he came alive again.

Various manifestations are possible when we take

the place of the dead with our minds. Amnesia is a common one, as pointed out above, and it takes on many different forms. Another is memory loss, a kind of dying of the stored data in the bank. Still another comes in the shape of confusion, where things get scrambled and uncertain. Future research on brain pathology as related to this problem could contribute much to our understanding.

The sexual dimension

One of the most troublesome areas in holding to the dead is the sexual. This kind of "death"—identifying with a lost loved one—doesn't always get into the sex feelings but it can happen. I have already pointed out instances in the early years when death fear is used to control the sex impulses of children.

I am in position to give numerous case histories where frigid women and impotent men had unresolved grief problems. My own research into the area is convincing enough to keep me working on a better understanding of the relationship of death to frigidity and to impotence. The following case is typical:

A woman of thirty-seven called me in a panic, wanting to see me ahead of her scheduled time. She said she had suddenly learned that she was going to die. I worked out a time for her to come in early. She reported she had gone to her father's grave in Arizona, as I suggested, to deal with her unfinished grief.

While at the cemetery she became fully aware of the fact that her father was dead. Then in her feelings it followed that one day she would occupy an adjacent grave. This was the first time she had ever really felt she was a mortal human being, given to disease and demise. This awareness put her into panic which lasted until I could help her get her defenses up some-what—not, mind you, by trying to help her deny death, but by helping her accept it a little before covering it over.

The discussion of her father led to the problem of her sexual frigidity. Her particular fear was expressed in a twofold manner: she feared the full release of orgasm would make her breathless and she would die. Then she feared if she didn't die, her husband would. She didn't know which she feared most, dying herself or killing her husband.

The above case had some complications from earlier years. Her father was a weak man who slept with her whenever her mother went to social affairs; she remembered some overstimulation. Then her father walked in on her petting a boy at the age of fourteen. He threatened her with total rejection if he ever caught her doing that again. She got the idea that all boy-girl contact had to be cut off. This lasted for several years, but she could never forget the prohibition her father laid on her sex feelings: in her feelings there was the fear that sex would bring death.

I would not say that her father's death caused the frigidity; that pattern was already set. But her mixed feelings about him served to perpetuate for her the problem of his death. After the session reported above, the woman's hands became extremely warm, whereas before her hands had always been cold. She began to move toward a solution of her frigidity although that is likely to take some time in view of the long years spent in a set pattern.

It is worthy of our attention that children do get *sex* and *death* mixed together. Where they come up with the assumption that sex will bring death, is it any wonder that sex scares them to death as adults? A man who had this fear of death in his sex feelings had adolescent fantasies of copulating with a dead body. It should not be surprising that this fear could pervert the sex drive so that at its extreme it could require some sort of human sacrifice. In the Middle Ages this sort of thing was associated with witchcraft and sorcery. That we haven't gotten completely beyond it is borne out when we read of mass sex murders in Houston, Texas, where twenty-seven lives were consumed to gratify these perverted impulses.[2]

I will venture the assumption that if we can get death out of sex, it can return to its intended purpose of creating life instead of consuming it. This statement is not a blanket indictment of homosexuals; I

---

[2] *Time*, Aug. 20, 1973, p. 24.

accept them as persons and am not seeking to condemn. Rather I am speaking of the end results of perversion of the sex drive, of those situations where the perversion is allowed to run its full course. Certainly, not all perversion of sex is homosexual in nature; heterosexual expression too is perverted when it requires suffering (and potentially a sacrifice) for its consummation.

3.
Death of a Relationship

The most stubborn grief in existence—living grief —deals with lost relationships. Where a real death is difficult to accept, its finality does help with acceptance. But the loss of a relationship can be held in fantasy, in hope, in dream that one day there might be a restoration. So much energy and vitality is drained off that a person can put himself only partly into family, work, and social relationships. He finds it difficult to invest fully in vacation, fun, travel or whatever, because he is trapped by his memories and finds himself unable to give them up.

Lost Relationships of Childhood

Most often the lost relationships of childhood revolve around a parent. In a divorce and separation from one of the parents the one that goes away is the ideal one; the one that stays with the children is the real one. The fantasies don't usually fix on the one at hand, but the absent one.

A boy who got separated from his mother worked feverishly at sports as an adolescent, hoping she would read of his successes in the newspapers. All this was to say, "Look, Mama, I deserve your love. Won't you read about me and be proud of me; write to me and let me know where you are and tell me that I matter to you?" But she never read the papers! Though he never heard from her, he kept on as an adult, hoping there would be a reunion by her initiation.

A girl, separated from her father in a divorce, tried everything to attract his love. He married again and became a "father" to one of her girl friends, but he paid no attention to his daughter. He sent her no money, gave her no presents and didn't show up for her wedding. Still she hoped, worked, struggled, prayed, but couldn't accept the fact that her father would have nothing to do with her. Her marriage didn't last, none of her relationships were satisfying because they were all "seconds"; none of them were as important as the possible love of her father.

A ten-year-old boy watching his mother leave on the bus tugged at her dress and begged her not to get on. But she left. His father took care of him, but he had no warmth for his father; his memories of him were of harshness, impatience and frugality. The boy grew up and married. He lived with the fear that his wife would leave him. He had promised himself that he would never be left again by a woman. This obsessive fear of his wife's leaving finally became more than she could endure, and she left. His only option was to take his life because he couldn't bear to repeat the pain he had felt at ten.

Parental relationships are not the only ruptured childhood relationships that bring prolonged grief, of course, but they are by far the most frequent. The intensity of the grief usually results from not getting the blessing of the one from whom it was so earnestly sought.

Occasionally brothers and sisters will carry an imaginary attachment or love if they are separated from one another. The problem is intensified where twins are parted. And it frequently happens between cousins separated by moving after there was extreme closeness. Edgar Allan Poe's *Annabel Lee* is the expression of the strength of a childhood love—one child for a neighbor child.

One of the most powerful situations of prolonged grief comes where "class" and social position forces the breakup of a childhood attachment. The poor boy goes out and does well to prove to "her" parents that he was worthy after all. He may live all his life proving his worth. A little white girl couldn't let her love be shown for the son of the maid and she "proved" her love by going as a missionary to Africa.

Lost Relationships in Adolescence

The loss of parents through divorce and separation can be a powerful thing to an adolescent, but it is seldom as strong as the loss in earlier years, especially from three to ten or eleven.

During adolescence many attachments are made and broken. Where there is a traumatic break between boy and girl, the fantasy goes to work to deny the pain, to absolve blame, to soothe the hurt. Unless the break is resolved to mutual satisfaction, a boy or girl can establish so strong a fixation on the lost one that it can be a lifelong fantasy. In some cases, a girl matures faster than her lover and begins to reach for the company of older boys. A boy can date another girl at a vacation spot or at different schools, causing the lover to break off because of jealousy. Parents may interfere, interests can become divergent, educational lags can disrupt, or professional studies can absorb too much concern. The old problems of class, race, religion, ethnic background, politics and social interests all come in for their share of ruptured relationships. Where the injured lover can't give up his injury, a situation of grief can sometimes last a life-time.

When such a relationship can't be solved, the injured person can go on to act "as if" he were moving through life in the same way as his peers. But though he goes on to new courtships, no woman in heaven or on earth can compare to the fantasy lover. He actually longs for what might have been, and he lives his life as if he will finally get back to what he missed. Unfortunately, this fantasizing can go on even after marriage, family, and grandchildren.

Lost Relationships in Adult Life

Much depression in adults may go back to former losses, even all the way back to early childhood. But adults go through the same kind of loss that children and adolescents suffer.

A husband and wife with four children formed a close friendship with another couple. In the course of time the husband of the second couple appeared at their home in a poetic and romantic mood, telling his friend's wife how beautiful, how wonderful, how feminine she was. This was the kind of thing her own husband had never done; in fact no man had said all these flattering things to her. She invested her affection in this man and had an affair with him. Eventually her husband got a promotion and was moved to a new place. She went with him, but for some ten years the "lover" lingered in her mind as the great happening. She was cured of her fantasy only when her lover came to see her and revealed that he had become an alcoholic; she gave up her dreams about him after she saw him in a drunken stupor.

Attempts to Solve Living Grief

Not many situations end with the good fortune of the case just described. That woman was fortunate to see the real humanity of the man she had so completely idealized.

If we are victims of a fantasy, or if we have an unreal attachment to the past, we need to look at two things: our need to have a fantasy and our prospects for success if we follow the course we have chosen.

Our need for fantasy

Need for a fantasy could come from our reluctance to deal with our reality. Fantasy keeps us from intimacy. Maybe we would rather dream of a perfect relationship than take the risk of establishing the best relationship we are able in the now. In addition we might be modeling or identifying with a parent or grandparent who was hung up in fantasy, couldn't invest, and therefore didn't teach us how to take the risks of reality. Sometimes a person will hold to a fantasy as if it were the only toy left from childhood or the only storybook from the nursery.

But reality is more rewarding than fantasy—if we

will only invest in it and be true to what it teaches us, even from its pains.

But there is no way to go if we cannot take our investment of feelings out of the past or out of the unreachable present. There is no way to withdraw the investment unless we can do what is necessary to finish the relationship. As long as we feed it, it will live; it has lived only on what we have fed it. Why do we keep on feeding it?

Each person can search out what he must do to put an end to his fantasy. But it will not die easily. It takes an act of will, a will to bring it to an end. One woman in a group dynamics situation came to the time when each person was asked to write on a piece of paper what he or she felt must be given up. She finally got the courage to write her father's name on the paper. The papers were then collected and burned. With that symbolic act she began to give up the dream of getting her father's love and blessing, and gradually she became able to invest in her husband and children what she took back from her father.

Sometimes the fantasy goes away when it can be shared with a trusted friend. This is not always a solution; that depends on the person, the situation.

The chance for success

In looking at the chance for success I have used F. S. Perls's idea of "permission" to help break up impossible dreams. A married man with a family was still idealizing his former adolescent sweetheart, who had also married and had a family. She had taken the initiative to break up their relationship in favor of a graduate student. He had seen her a few times since but she showed absolutely no interest in any way in returning to the past. She had her life, her husband, her friends and she seemed happy. I asked him to have his dream, to go ahead and work it out. The more he worked on it the more he saw that this was not what he really wanted and he knew she didn't want a change. But in talking out his fantasy he was able to grieve and give it up, a process that required quite a lot of suffering on his part. The thing that symbolized his last hold on her was a handkerchief. I asked him to bring it to me. I took out a book of matches and handed it to him without saying a word. He wept bitterly, he wrung the handkerchief, he kissed it, he stroked it, and finally with great reluctance he struck a match and set it on fire. He was on his way! I don't know if he could have won his freedom without that act.

One has to ask what most symbolizes such a relationship, and he has to *act* to get rid of that symbol. I couldn't burn the handkerchief for the man; he had to burn it, and it had to be his *choice* to do so. Such a symbol can be a lock of hair, a picture, a batch of letters, a fountain pen, a locket, a ring, a poem, or a garment. It can be a place, a ritual, a habit or a song.

Each person can find a symbol if he has the courage to look. And that can be a starting place.

The Death of a Hope

One of the griefs we carry may not be attached to a person so much as to a hope. We count on our relationships to be fulfilled through a hope or projected plan of life.

It seems that Jesus had a hope that he built into his dreams and plans from childhood. To rid his family of the curse and stigma around the circumstances of his birth he took on himself the hopes of his family; maybe his doing so could also be a way to lift the blight of poverty from them. And because the people of Israel harbored a hope for fulfillment through the Messiah's coming, he could put parental wish together with national longings and strive toward a worthwhile existence.

The temptations in the wilderness are a biography of a death: the death of a whole set of hopes, wishes, dreams, longings and aspirations. Everything of the past had to be thrown out. Perhaps this was where Jesus got in touch with both death and rebirth. He learned what it was to shake off every article and every trapping that supported his dreams. With this kind of devastating emptying, there came the most impossible filling. He seemed to touch the point where neither nature nor spirit can tolerate the vacuum, and there came rains in the desert.

When the Apostle Paul suddenly encountered the Spirit of Jesus, the Spirit was able to strip him of all his former structures that might have led him to power, influence, and prominence. Then, he said, he was able to call them dung, fertilizer, or rot that would support new life. The principle at work is the death of childhood (and carnal, nonspiritual) hope that becomes a corpse: from this the spiritual man makes a beginning.

PART II

Toward a Method and Reason
in Healing from Death

4.
Grief Therapy

This chapter is written especially for counselors and those who help with grief problems. It will be useful also in providing careful readers with heightened insights for dealing with grief in many areas.

Before one can begin work on the solution of a grief problem, say, in an adult, it is most important to distinguish the three kinds of grief already dealt with in the earlier chapters of this book:

1) The childhood terror: getting life out of death.
2) The adult loss: getting death out of life.
3) Lost relationships: self-recriminations over the relationship before death occurred.

Main emphasis will be on the first two categories.

The Childhood Terror: Getting Life
Out of Death

An adult who loses a meaningful person by death tends to replay childhood fears and phobias associated with his first introduction to the matter of death and dying. This material comes through on a different emotional track from the plain hurt over separation that results in clinging to the dead in some way or other. The third zone or track may also be present, bringing into focus the painful loss of a past that can never be recovered: that past is powerfully represented by the death of one whose existence was interwoven with the past.

Signs that strongly indicate the childhood reaction to death are readily apparent when one knows what to look for. The following may reveal such:

» Fear to touch the dead.

» Reluctance to enter into plans for the funeral.

» Haste in getting the funeral finished, such as a hurry to set the burial date as soon as possible.

» Getting so busy with arrangements and looking after all the particulars to the degree that one does not slow up to grieve.

» Resistance to viewing the remains, even requiring no opening of the casket at the funeral.

» Inability to be at the bedside at the time of death, or hurrying away as soon as possible when it occurs.

» Inability to find tears or reluctance to let others cry.

» Moving to the center to support all others who mourn and finding usefulness in being a kind of family priest upon whom the others lean. This becomes a rationalization that one must hold up in order to let everybody else become dependent; the one doing the supporting can delay his own grief.

» Becoming faint, chilly or withdrawn. This sign that one can't cope with the childhood feelings was illustrated earlier by the woman who said, when her mother died, "I felt that all the warmth had gone out of the world." In another case of this sort a woman who lost her father needed a coat on a hot July night.

» Showing too much haste in returning to normal routines of home and work, e.g., returning to the regular TV viewing the evening following the funeral.

» Inability to allow others to give strong support at the time of greatest need.

» Relying on medication to prolong the shock of grief.

» Tears in the night, especially the repetition of frightening dreams.

» Struggling to breathe, tightness in the chest, stoppage of nasal passages or the bronchial tubes. All these are sometimes childhood identifications with the horror of death.

» Numbness in parts of the body such as the extremities, a simulation of death.

» Fear of enclosures such as elevators and small rooms. Such fears can be an identification with the tight enclosure of the casket, and hence a way of avoiding the ultimate.

Other more everyday examples of death denial come in acting a younger age, looking a younger age, dressing to appear younger, identifying with the children in behavior and at parties, overlooking birthdays. The same denial shows itself in not attending funerals, not accepting what the mirror reveals, and being in a constant search for the fountain of youth. The list can continue: not taking out adequate life insurance, not planning for the future, ignoring making a will or normal estate planning.

These situations are just a few of many that indicate how an adult can deny the actual impact of death. Usually traceable to childhood terror, the adult's reaction indicates he is still too frightened to allow the reality of death to come through to his feelings. In sitting on the childhood stuff, all adult grief is also blocked.

In the loss of a parent, the "adult" in us needs to cry and the "child" needs to cry. The adult could weep, but wouldn't want his child of the past to cry: that would be too embarrassing to one's image of himself. The helper needs to be able to allow the child to come to the surface and weep, shudder and become overwhelmed.

No two people develop the childhood psychology of death the same way. But in one way or another, it is there in the basic notion that death kills whatever it touches. This childhood psychology is frequently so strong it can override adult sensibilities and bring back the old fears. But when we can get these things out of the past and out into the light, the adult can teach the child. The path of repression and of refusing to ventilate unacceptable feelings guarantees that the adult will not grow much in his experiences of grief.

Whatever irrational fears or inadequate explanations the child learned he will still be carrying until they are updated. And the best time to make the proper corrections is in an adult experience that will allow the corrections to be made:

If there was the assumption that death had some strange power to move, to become ghostly, shadowy or to stalk after midnight, you can be sure that some of it remains in the feelings.

If death had some imagined ability to communicate with the living, this will persist in strange ways.

If the dead had some imagined ability to put a curse on the living there will be some kind of dread about the whole business of the wake and the funeral.

If death was thought the point where God comes to take a person, religious ministrations may be tolerated but may not be appreciated.

If the resolve in the child was to deny his own

mortality, the adult will work every trick to deny the death of a parent, grandparent or other loved one that could make him suddenly a generation older. All funerals will be avoided because the gathering of friends under such circumstances is one of the better ways available to all of us to help keep us in touch with the aging process.

Whatever the unresolved childhood feelings happened to be, any helper will have to show the courage to open the grave of the past, as it were, so the grave can be closed in the present. This will mean rather constant communication and contact, once there is a passage opened to the past. If closeness in following up is not observed, there can be a sudden flight away from the terror and the game could be lost.

The following are some situations that are characteristic but by no means exhaustive:

There was the death of a father where a seven-year-old boy, the oldest of three children, was admonished to become the "man of the house." He got the horror of death without getting to the pain of the separation. In adult life he didn't want to go back and open up the old wound which was necessary if he was going to grow.

The death of a father for a six-year-old boy meant separation from his mother because she couldn't take care of all her children. Death meant double loss and he couldn't cope with its fears when he became an adult.

An eight-year-old lost her only other sibling, a sister of six, when she burned to death. The mother constantly reminded the living child that fire took the wrong one. She was so imprinted with a need to "give her life" that the whole matter of death was a constant threat. She lived with a compulsion to avoid anything that reproduced the horror scene. A television news report of people burning in a fire was enough to hospitalize her.

A four-year-old boy lost his mother, who was buried in a family plot adjacent to the backyard. His curiosity about the grave was such that he became an archeologist, digging every grave he could explore in Egypt and the Middle East.

Sigmund Freud blacked out at the funeral of his father. He interpreted the reaction to be a result of his childhood rivalry toward his father for his mother's tenderness. That was only part of the story, I feel, but Freud gave us no material from his early years on which to base further conclusions.

There are situations where a child loses a parent or grandparent after wishing the event, thus injecting special terror into the picture coupled with a fear of one's power. In the adult years a fear may result that one must be careful with all feelings lest the love or the anger could bring catastrophe. At age three a man lost his father to a sudden heart attack. At thirteen he lost his stepfather the same way. When he was thirty-five, the death of President Kennedy gave him the dreadful fear that he caused it even though he was in Chicago when the assassination occurred in Dallas. At age five Friedrich Nietzsche, an only son, lost his father. Perhaps it is scarcely a wonder that in his later years he announced the "death of God." It gives us cause to ponder the appearance of "Death of God" theology the year following President Kennedy's death. The Nietzsche in many of us was stirred to memory.

A lady had lost her little brother when she was six. She lost her father when she was twenty-eight. Then a brief illness of her husband brought her feelings to the surface to say, "I seem to kill everything I love." In other words she felt it was dangerous to let her love loose. She needed to have her childhood fears updated so she could be free to love without the fear of killing.

In these and many cases, the adult needs to return to the childhood scene in order to truly become an adult. Help from the counselor comes in his willingness and ability to get the life out of death—the death the child has imposed on life under conditions of horror and terror. When this can be done the next stage of grief can be managed with much greater benefit: the stage of getting death out of life.

Getting Death Out of Life

The parallel track in adult grief is the one that must deal with the loss of this particular person.

Taking the place of the dead is a common occurrence. Death leaves an emptiness that demands filling. When the grieving Roman mob weeps for Caesar, Shakespeare has one commoner cry out, "Let Brutus be Caesar." We seem to feel that somebody should volunteer his life on the occasion of death, by throwing himself into the empty space. Who will sit in the chair, sing the songs, write the letters, give the commands, offer the tenderness, observe the festivals, or stroke the dog? The one who is unable to observe the vacuum and wait is the volunteer for filling the emptiness. The oldest son is the likely candidate for the father, the oldest daughter for the mother. The other children permit it; often encourage it. When this happens grief is cut short and the dead is taken into one's life; and the process kills. We can't identify with the dead without starting to die prematurely.

Shunning the grief and loss is another way of making sure that death will be incorporated in the living. Grief gets death out, while an absence of grief internalizes the process and psychologically the burial takes place inside the living.

Exceptional circumstances may block the proper progress of grief. For example, mutilation of the body by fire or accident can delay the process. Loss of a son in the war can leave parents uncertain of the beginning and ending of grief.

A woman planned that her body be given to a medical school with a memorial service instead of a regular funeral. Although this provision insured that the children would have less grief at the time of her death, the grief was spread over years as a result.

Another exceptional circumstance comes in a greatly prolonged death such as a stroke or cancer. All the family waits and waits for the end that is too slow in coming. They have grieved much, but cannot grieve at the end because of the relief. Sometimes the final burst of awareness and acceptance is delayed for months or years because there was no room for tears at the time of the funeral.

Transfer to objects is a common way of delaying grief. In John Steinbeck's *To a God Unknown* the "spirit" of the father is assumed to be in a giant oak tree, which the sons look on as a living symbol of the deceased father. A little girl looked on her dead father as living in the dog he loved most; as long as the dog lived, her father lived. A herdsman was alive to his children in a herd of Black Angus cattle. Such a transfer can take place in objects of the home, especially heirlooms. Whatever the deceased loved can represent him and the denial of his death continues. This can be a vase, a piano, a rug, a uniform, an automobile, a chair, a painting, a clock, or a book, especially a Bible.

Assuming a task can delay grief. Some deceased people who had a job before them as their way of making a name bequeath the unfinished work to all their loved ones. But the inheritance becomes a curse to fall upon uncooperative sons, daughters, friends who fail to give money and energy to the espoused cause. They must give up their own right to exist in order to do what the deceased left for them as a task. Grief then is inappropriate because the task is there to be done, and the living are overwhelmed by what they feel is required of them. The dead thus inhabits the living by requiring energy to be expended in completing some unfinished task.

Reading of the will can sometimes be the place where grief gets blocked. A man who left all his land to his son and only a few scattered articles of little worth to his daughter hurt and angered her so by his flagrant partiality that she couldn't mourn.

Arguments over partiality will often throw the children of the deceased parent into consternation. One daughter started a fight in the room where her father expired, saying, "I loved him most." This angered the other daughters to the point that they got all the way through the funeral with no show of grief.

Religious differences can prevent grief from being expressed. Arguments can boil up over the church and consequent place of burial, who will conduct the funeral, what preacher the deceased might have wanted or not wanted, and the like.

The helper must be prepared for these and a thousand other obstructions that block the grief process. When grief is interrupted or blocked, there is invariably a problem of holding to the dead—of getting death into life! Life cannot function around a lump of death, at least not very well. Where death is worked through and accepted, it brings great renewal to the living. Where it is shunned, evaded or denied, the psychology of its power arises to put a curse on the living.

Any attempt to spare the pain and core of the suffering comes short of what people need. They need to get to the heart of it and cut loose from obligations, guilts, fears, tasks, memories or dreads that take away their right to personhood and freedom, including the right to be angry and the right to love, no matter what. Nobody owes the dead his life; if one feels such obligation, it is certainly a misplaced obligation.

Technique or method is not so important as the knowledge that we need the death purged from our spirits. As long as death is felt to be the great enemy, we are overlooking the impact of the basic gift of the gospel. That gift is the assertion of a faith that as nature takes death as a bonus, so the spirit of man can be enriched by death . . . if death is accepted. Where death is not accepted, it remains a kind of curse. But death is seldom an enrichment at first.

Death of Opportunity and Relationships

There is a kind of dying to the human spirit where lost relationships are not accepted. First, there is the loss of time, coupled with the denial that time has passed. Second, there is the loss of opportunity that cannot be recovered, and, third, there is the loss of association with vital and meaningful persons. The third is actually pretty much mixed up with the first two problems.

The loss of time is a special grief, and there's no grief more poignant than the loss of childhood. You can't go home again; much of mystery has gone out of life; you can't recapture innocence; there is no more Santa Claus; the Mary Poppins world of magical cause is only a fond memory; a place called Camelot with King Arthur and his Knights of the Round Table is only a "once upon a time": the midnight hour has struck and turned our carriages all to pumpkins. The loss of time is inevitable, but we compound the problem in spending even more time trying to open the door back to the world of innocence and magic. In our anxiety we deal with the past as though we could change it, and we neglect the future—the only place where change is possible, and the only area where growth is possible. An effective helper is one who can bring a person to accept the idea that the past is the past, that it cannot be changed, that its doors are shut, sealed and barred. Only then can a person take the future seriously as opportunity. But be careful—if we take the future as necessity, we will be operating in a philosophy of despair. If the future can be chosen, it becomes open to creative and meaningful relationships.

The loss of opportunity keeps us living in the regret that we have failed our moment. It was all there for us and we didn't see it: we could have bought that property, could have gone to college, might have married the one we loved, could have taken the job that led to success and money. All these regrets tend to be a way of saying that there will be no further need of striving, the good chances were missed and there's no way to recover and go on to success, love, accomplishment or service.

The loss of vital and meaningful relationship to persons covers a wide area of associations. We regret that we muffed the ball, blundered in our choices, or were too stupid to read the right signals. We may wish that we had the old high school gang together again; those were the good times, but the present has no such enjoyment or delight. Unfortunately, such attitudes make former times great, but only create despair over the present.

5.
The Knowledge of Mortality

As a five-year-old child, I learned an unforgettable thing in the death and burial of a neighbor. I learned about and I felt the awfulness of "no air in the coffin." It gave me chills and shudders to put myself in the place of the dead man. You have to do that just once to get the full horror picture. This is a knowledge that is in a category by itself.

Most knowledge acts on us in some way or other, but the knowledge that we are really mortal, limited, finite and corruptible sends us into a spin to do something. There are many possible responses, but the usual one is denial and repression, or perhaps evasion and avoidance. We say to ourselves that such misery must not become permanent! We can't forever keep gazing on the glassy eye or the pallid cheek of death. As a child I felt an impelling force driving me away from that dreadful sight, and I vowed never to return.

But now, as an adult, I declare my freedom from my childhood resolve. I want to, I must move on and deal with what the knowledge of being mortal does to mortals.

Not all knowing implies doing, as Socrates thought. To teach truth does not guarantee that those taught will follow it. Knowledge may or may not act on persons, and on the other hand, persons may or may not respond to what they learn.

I can learn some things just for the sake of learning them. This may be true of historical facts, aesthetic truth, mathematical formulae, geographical information, and a whole host of other areas like geology, ecology, theology, psychology, finance, meteorology, philosophy. It is true that some of this information may excite me, frighten me, drive me or stall me. Some of it I seek just to help explain my experiences and interpret my particular pilgrimage. Some of it I will seek to better my condition and the condition of those around me.

The Knowledge That Has Power

Most knowledge seems to give me the choice of seeking it or not. Usually I seek it for a given purpose and it furthers that purpose as I use it. Most knowledge does not act on me so as to drive me by its own force. But the knowledge of mortality does exactly that. In it we identify with all mortals: it strikes at the gut level and forces us into startling awareness of our physical destiny.

Seen in this light, the Garden of Eden story speaks to me with new emphasis. I assume that there was a certain knowledge that led to "sin." The knowledge that was fully discovered was the knowledge that man was man, not God, and therefore limited by time and circumstance. By eating the forbidden fruit and crossing his external limits, man discovered his internal limits—his mortal boundaries. One forbade him to return to a position of not-knowing (innocence). The other would not let him "be as God" and thus exempt him from moving toward wrinkles, arthritis, heart disease, grey hair, digestive upset, disability, death and decay.

I do not assume that the *knowledge* of mortality is the *cause* of mortality. The child is born as a mortal creature, but only comes to know that he is mortal when he experiences the fact that the others around him die, and he identifies with just one of them. Then he knows it really. And he can never forget it. Maybe he would be able to forget if it happened just once, but the act repeats itself endlessly, and each act reminds him that his own nature is a part of all the others.

Death becomes power knowledge to the child when he identifies with a body in the casket and watches dirt being shoveled into the grave. He imagines the terrors of that breathless existence and feels the boundaries closing in. He sees skeletons and he knows. One of my children queried, "Do you mean I've got one of those inside me?" and then concluded, "It makes me scared of myself."

Perhaps much of the history of a person can be written around the power of his knowledge of mortality to impel him to action. This shouldn't necessarily make us morbid. Morbidity occurs when people can't get anything else going. On the other hand, foolishness sets in when a person can't allow the limits of mortality to speak their reality. The buffoon and the clown try to act out a complete denial of human mortality while the depressed or despairing person lives as if the ultimate limits were already upon him.

Human life derives its flavor from recognizing the limits without constantly being enslaved by them. Human acceptance of mortality means on the one hand that I cannot absorb myself in pure animal existence where there is no opportunity to get outside myself and observe the process. On the other hand, it means that I don't go around like Hamlet, always contemplating cutting the strings that bind me to the process so I can be free by "shuffling off this mortal coil." The wish to return to animal (to innocence and not-knowing, as it once was) or to rise completely above the mortal limits (the Tower of Babel) is not a possibility, Pascal reminds us. But herein lies our temptation to sin. We want to return or to go on, and in either case we deny what it means to be human— to live life somewhere within the boundaries, to live life "in the meantime."

The pressure of the boundaries acts as a spring for human motivation. Without this pressure, life would collapse as a lung without air. The boundaries are constant reminders of the nature of our pilgrimage, lending both character and sweetness to it. The poet is not understood unless we know that he reflects everything against the boundary or the limits of our existence. The musician finds the sorrow there to sweeten his melody. The artist painting the sunset touches the same note with the stroke of a brush. We are reminded and nudged a bit by birthdays, the falling of the leaves, the scream of the siren, the lowing of cattle at sundown, the lonesome baying of the hound, the ruins of some old plantation house.

I am affirming that the deep awareness of death— my own death—is a powerful knowledge that moves me. This is *the* knowledge that drives me to action; it is the knowledge that addresses me and reveals me to myself in ways I never asked to be revealed. It rips away my defenses: the knowledge of death is shattering, devastating, chilling, frightening.

There is no impelling knowledge on the opposite

side that leads to faith as the knowledge of death leads to sin and desperation, to guilt and anxiety. I affirm that the sin comes in what I do because I don't want to accept the full knowledge of mortality. Sin is my act of denying mortality, or changing it, or distorting it, or in some way getting something going that will serve as a diversion. The denial and the diversion can be the story of my earthly and human journey.

Death ultimately says that I am powerless to avoid the erosion of time upon my physical existence.

When death knowledge sends the child to his parents with unanswered questions many parents tend to take the easy way out. They put all this unresolved data over onto the church, religion, and God. Then these become a part of the denial of death rather than a help with it. Telling the child, "Your uncle has gone to be with Jesus," has the unfortunate result of making Jesus a glorified collector of dead people. His touch to the child means death, not life.

So often the first uses of religion in the child's history are connected with some sort of denial of the awfulness of death. It is as if religion is brought onto the scene to say, "Cheer up, we do have an answer for this thing," and if we did have one, the child couldn't apply it any way except as a kind of palliative for the idea of "corruption" or a denial of the seeming permanence of the grave.

The paradox is that we offer the child a solution

to death, namely God, and God then is put over in the death category. So if God gives "life," it is a bloodless, skeletal, spooky existence, and it is frightening.

For centuries, the power of God, represented in the Spirit, has been popularly known as "Holy Ghost." For the child, if there is one thing more to be feared than an ordinary ghost it is a "holy" one. A ghost is conceived to have all too much power and wisdom, but let God and ghosts get together and you've got an unbeatable and dreadful combination.

Let me emphasize that unless we find ways to break the unconscious link between death and religion, then religion will continue to be the main force by which we deny death. Indeed in dragging religion in to rescue people from the horror of death, we don't get rid of that horror but spread it onto religion. It is as if you used a blanket to put out a fire, but instead of putting the fire out, you ignited the blanket.

We said the knowledge of death leads to sin—the desperate act or plan to deny or change the facts. We also affirm that there is no contrasting knowledge that drives one to faith. But where faith leads to acceptance of death and mortality, a "Spirit" knowledge arises and drives out the childhood terror.

If I could accept resurrection in a completely trusting way, then that knowledge might have some imperative in it for me. But because I am not constituted so that I can know for sure, the concept of resurrec-

tion calls for faith; it is not given as a certainty. Even
if it is given to someone else as experience, I still must
move into death hoping, trusting, but not knowing.

The knowledge of death, on the other hand, does
not come as something I must have faith in. I don't
need to trust in death: it is a certainty. The knowledge of death presents me with an imperative, not a
call to trust it. The imperative is the binding fact of
the ubiquity of death: "All flesh is as grass," or, "This
too shall pass away."

The perception of my mortality, my human limits,
my corruptibility, all represent the *power* of death.
This pervasive power makes the architect build, the
poet write, the musician sing, and the prophet warn.
It is a pressure that acts on all our means, all our
actions. It is not the only theme of culture, but a central theme that is never silenced.

Perhaps much of the power of death is imaginary
on our part. (Where would the world of man be
without death?) In any case, the state of death is
motionless, silent and actually physically powerless.
In the face of that fact, we humans put up quite a
struggle to avoid or delay our rendezvous with the
end-time.

Death speaks the most absolute "no" that we know
about. It says we cannot cross the limits to make contact with one we love under any circumstances, no
matter what methods we use, either scientific or religious. It defines the border beyond which there is no

trespassing. We can even research the process of dying in order to make this knowledge useful, yet we can't research death. We have no data on that final experience. Indeed this is the big experience that gathers all lesser experiences into itself.

The "no" and the absolute denial of death stands as life's chief frustration. We have devised no method for getting into it with reportable results, nor any effective detour around it. My own personal experience of incomparable frustration and anger as a five-year-old is still borne out in my repeated encounters with death in a hospital setting. From my experience there, it is my judgment that the dread the physician has in bringing the word of death to relatives results from seeing the frustration and anger that it immediately produces—emotions not always verbalized, but usually present, and ready to gush.

Humanity, Mortality, and Jesus

Are we going too far afield if we assume that the message of death only touches anger and frustration that we all tend to carry all the time? That this or that experience of death simply stirs again what most of us felt when first we were stabbed with the truth about our human mortality?

Each experience of loss can be a stern reminder that I can't repress my original pain about the whole sordid business of death.

If mortality and humanity go together, my greatest temptation will be essentially one of denying my humanity in order to rid myself of my fears and frustrations over mortality.

Although there is no way a human can research scientifically the facts of death per se, I want to offer the thing I consider closest to it. And that closeness is not one of finding a man with cancer and following him step by step through the process, as important as that may be in contributing to our knowledge. There are other ways in which persons go through a kind of death. The closest thing to physical death, it seems to me, is the event or experience that blocks out every goal and purpose that a person holds dear to himself. There is a kind of death when one is publicly humiliated, when a major investment goes sour, one's company goes bankrupt, one's team loses the big game, or when one gets defeated in a major political campaign.

This theme was central to the experience of Jesus. As a result, he sought to bless life by taking away some of the power of death to rob persons of value.

In Jesus' encounter with John the Baptist (at baptism) I take it that Jesus had already spent some eighteen years trying to put together an "office" for messiahship in Israel. I also take it that he couldn't put it together in any of the ways and methods he had hoped to use. He was faced with an ordeal of "temptations" to make his life into an exception or an exemption from the ordinary human plight that is essentially bound up with being mortal. Either he couldn't or wouldn't put his messiahship together along the line of these exceptional possibilities. He "denied" himself the right to be anybody but Jesus of Nazareth, mortal and limited. The experience was a death of deep proportions and followed by forty days of fasting (and dying). What came out of that "death" is what Jesus has to communicate to me: that I can die to what or who I want most. Granted, I never had an offer like he had, but I am not called on to die his death, but rather the one that has my name on it.

"Spirit" knowledge is the new knowledge of life that comes from our "resurrection" in our own little wilderness, wherever or whatever that is.

When Jesus emerged from the wilderness and called his disciples it was with the intent of setting the stage finally for them to die to their hopes of a "Kingdom" for which they longed and dreamed. In fact he became the focal point of their hope, but all the while he told them there was no kingdom as they understood it.

In losing Jesus, they lost their earthly hope and had to die to that loss. When they got "Spirit" knowledge (after forty days of waiting), we are told they counted it a privilege to suffer as a price for having known Jesus, and they would sooner die than give up the value and vitality of this experience.

Perhaps it is not too bold an assumption to make that the disciples had their own human problems in dealing with their mortality. Perhaps they wanted to use Jesus to help them avoid or deny their problem. He refused to lead them along such a path; instead he kept the flash card of his own mortality before them.

His concern, to my own way of thinking, was not one of establishing "resurrection life" as an after-mortal-death experience, but of letting them die to their personal hopes and dreams for a more immediate purpose: that they might enter life and celebration now in such a way that they could trust God with the future. Their new faith produced a knowledge resulting in positive action for living far stronger than the power of the fear of death had to bring denial and evasion. They were able to affirm that the life powers of faith were indeed blessing enough to overcome the childhood shadows of curse surrounding death and dying.

6.
Death and Time

Dealing with Time

In the morning time of the human race, our father Adam ate of the forbidden fruit—the fruit that would make one wise—and he saw more than he wanted to see. He saw that his time was limited, that he was mortal, and that he, like the birds and beasts, would have to drink the cup of mortality. His first impulse was to deny what he had seen. He covered his flesh so none of the decay would show.

He wanted to go back to the garden and forget what he had seen, but he was already a witness and there was no way now to return to innocence.

Was Adam made guilty by what he saw? Is it a sin to see what I am? Is it a sin for the child to see that he is mortal or for him to see that his parents are mortal? How is innocence lost? Was it different for Adam than it is for me? Is losing innocence the same thing as becoming guilty?

Perhaps Adam lost his innocence by what he saw just as a child loses his innocence when he sees an end-time for his parents and for himself. Childhood at least is lost this way. A child has already started being an adult when a funeral procession passes the gate of his garden of eternity. He can play some more, but an awesome referee begins to look in on his games. "Yet a little while," he says, "and you will have to stop and come inside."

How does guilt enter? Surely a child does not become guilty because he looks at the hard truth about his existence. Could it be in the thing the child imagines he has to do to overcome the fact of what he saw? Could it be in his denial of his mortal nature, and in his haste to erect some barrier between himself and the rapids in the stream ahead? Or could it be in his fruitless effort to put Humpty Dumpty together again? Could it be in his lifting up new gods who would be more lenient with time and more generous toward earth's pilgrims? Perhaps his mortal nature could be denied with good medicine and organ transplants, protected with better engineering, covered with polyester fiber, sweetened with 24-hour deodorants, decorated with jewels and filigree, transported in vehicles of style and power and nestled behind storehouses of tax-free bonds, burgeoning deep-freezes and comfortable bank balances. Does one need to listen to the trumpet of the angels or to fear the scythe of the grim reaper when he has double indemnity insurance, a series of sound medical check-ups, a generous retirement program and a good promotion coming up?

It seems to me that innocence is lost when the child has to deal with time. Time enters the picture as an enemy of life and of man. Time is traditionally portrayed in the image of an old man with a beard, reaping and gathering to himself all those who come within his reach. The game of life becomes one of cheating the reaper by any method at hand.

To the child, God is the keeper of time, identified with the old man with the beard. Adam saw him and wanted to deny him his power. He wanted the power over life (and death); he wanted to wrest the power from God because God became his enemy. Could this be Adam's guilt and mine? The guilt in not being able to accept that God is God? The guilt of hiding from time? The guilt of building a tower that would stand above the stream and give me a chance to ignore the valley of the shadow?

Perhaps it is not possible to see time until we are able to see its end. Time is a measure, a beat, a rhythm related to the diastole and cystole. When I have

enough imagination, I am able to project myself outside and above. This is where Adam gets above pure
animal existence and is able to see the whole stream.
At the same time that he gets above the stream, he
sees himself also as one of the swimmers. He cannot
fully get above and outside the process of human
existence. He is more like the flying fish who only
momentarily gets above it, only to fall back into the
waves and take his place with all the creatures being
swept along by the force of the flood.

My innocence is lost in seeing that I have a destiny
and an end not different from that of all other creatures. My guilt comes in my rejection of the natural
process. I don't want to be identified with all nature
and history. I want to be an exception on whatever
terms I can work out for myself. I want to swim
above the stream. I want to be a flying fish who remains above the water and the rapids.

In my desire for immortality I want to find the
hidden key and stand with God, to be as he is. If I
can't have this, my temptation is to plunge to the
depths of the water and identify with all the creatures
who never had a chance to see the process from the
outside. I would like to reimmerse myself into their
innocence and forget that there is either an end or a
beginning.

There is no way open for man to rise above the
stream and create his own immortality, and there is
no way for him to submerge himself in a forgetful-

ness of pure animal existence so that time is no longer a factor. He is forever a participant in the mortal flow and an observer just above it. He is no longer fully in it, nor fully above it. His sin comes on either side of the struggle: to get out of his humanity and mortality or to get lost in it.

Pascal says if I try to identify fully with God, I forget my humanity and become a victim of impossible pride. On the other hand if I identify only with the animal, I fall into despair. He says that in Jesus Christ is the *via media*, the middle way, because in him we see both God and our humanity (*Pensées*).

The psychology of man is essentially different from the psychology of animals because of *time*. No animal seems to struggle with time. He is in time to be sure, but is essentially as unaware of time as a bird is unaware of the air, or a fish is unconscious of the water.

The awareness of time marks man as the creature who is different. He is like all other creatures in that he is in the same stream with them, but he is different because he knows about the rapids downstream. A dog draws no meaning from another dog that has been killed by an automobile. He doesn't have the capacity to identify. But man has this ability. The dead man troubles us, he disturbs our peace, he gives us the creeps, he stirs our fears, he gives us nightmares. We identify with him to a degree, and we try to stop what we feel; we try to deny the pain and we ask for the support of living people to shake off this dreadful feeling.

A Psychology of Time

Our existence feels no challenge and no serious question until time enters our experience as a stranger and an enemy, bringing an abrupt halt to all that we are, all that we have and all we know. It is not internal to us to know of our end, but external. We don't naturally understand it and accept it. It is thrust upon us against our feelings and wishes. It comes as intruder and invader into our peaceful garden. We would rather not deal with it, but it will not go away. It moves in with the power to shatter the wholeness and innocence of our unbroken existence. When it enters there is no beginning and no end—therefore no middle, no now and then. The price of knowledge becomes very costly, even frightening. I must pay for it with my life when I had already felt life as endlessly extended. Time comes in with shock and rudeness and with the power to put limits around me that I didn't know about. When I thought my garden covered the earth, I learn about a fence, and, even worse, that I am outside and the gate is shut.

I can't totally experience time from the outside any more. I was once at home in the garden until a stranger passed and whispered the unwelcome truth.

All is changed by the message of that truth. I will have to deal with it as best I can, but forget that I heard it, I cannot. Time entered from the outside, and it gets inside gradually. Its beat and rhythm become the diastole and cystole of my being. I feel it in the falling leaves and in the sunset. I hear it in the winter wind and sense it in the scream of sirens, in the sight of wheelchairs and crutches, in the smell of rotting wood and the sight of an empty house. I hear it in the mournful lowing of cattle and the sorrowful notes of sweet music, in the rumble of a freight train at night and the howl of the lonesome coyote. This all says that nature knows but it does not know. And it says I know, and I know that I know.

God seems to choose to let us know something of what he knows, and yet not all of what he knows. Has he become our enemy in letting us have some of the knowledge? Is this the way he wakes us up to reality? Would any other message be enough to shake off our drowsiness and bring us to responsibility? God apparently chose not to let us remain children all our lives.

Is it possible that the truth about our end is intended to add sweetness to our lives rather than despair and bitterness? Do we really learn to value anything that comes in endless supply? Don't we really learn to value what is scarce and to love more completely that which we are losing?

The paradox of man comes in the fact that he grows from his frustration. He matures as he is able to accept his limits. Would any limit have meaning unless we ourselves were limited in time and space?

Isn't this the beginning of prayer and a search for God when his "no" is heard? Our quest for life becomes our question about life. Would there be a search if we had the answers?

Does the Christian have the answer to the big question? And the big question is how do I allow that God is God, and remain mortal, human, limited, powerless against the flow of time? To be sure we try to comfort ourselves with images of immortality. But the human and the animal in me does not welcome the event called my end. By nature I resist it and fight vigorously against it.

God seems to be saying that I can trust the future, the unknown, and the trip across the rapids. But in my little piece of history, there are no witnesses who have returned to say it is all okay, that God made it safe for them; and that he gave them some more time or another kind of time. How do I *know* there is *any* kind of survival? If there is no survival, what can I do about it?

Again, do we use Christianity and religion to guarantee some sort of survival after death?

I cannot accept that Jesus lived his life and died his death simply to give us a guarantee that we would survive the ultimate crash, nor to make us unsinkable

Molly Browns. The Christian faith is not to me a survival kit.

Perhaps the principle of survival or the notion of winning against death is contrary to the spirit of the Christ. I don't get the feeling that he went to the cross knowing his future. He did not cling to his life, but lived it in such a way that he was always turning it loose. He said the surest way to lose it was to cling to it. What I'm saying is not a new way to get a grip on life so we will never lose it. It is rather a way to surrender it, to let it go, to break our natural grip on it, to wrest ourselves from its stranglehold.

Christ celebrated life, he loved it, he lived it, he enjoyed it; he partied, he feasted, he loved; he lived life to the fullest; and he lost it.

If I must live the kind of life that assures my survival then I don't trust the words that say, "Because I live, you shall live." These words were not spoken to help men live, but rather to help them give up their lives. Somebody else will live for you, forget your own lives!

But my natural self says, "I want to live, I want to survive, I want to exist." The Christian faith comes back to say, give your lives over and up to the one who will live for you. But again, is that enough?

My demand to live, to survive and to be, becomes the greatest enemy of my living, surviving and being.

The truth of the New Testament is that we can't live unless we die. If we can't die, we can't live.

God has seemingly always said you can't know, you must wait. If you must know, you defeat everything related to faith.

Dying can be the greatest act of faith. I really don't know, for I have no road map through the valley. I have no company, no friends to walk along with me the whole distance. They must wait at the boundary.

Dying is not a community act, but a lonesome and lonely journey.

Paradoxically, Christianity is not first a method of dying, but a way of living and this includes giving up life.

In Jesus Christ God seemed to make a new invasion of *time*. Men had become slaves because of their fear of time—that is, death—and of God.

We do not want to "go to God." We want to delay the journey, because God is more identified with death than life, in our feelings.

We console our children with words like these: "Don't cry, Grandpa has gone to be with Jesus." The picture the child gets is that Jesus must have a powerfully icy grip. When he touches you, you are finished. The coming of Jesus is always pictured as the end of time, therefore as death. When the child grows a little, we challenge him to give his life to Jesus, and he has a set of thoughts quite different from his feelings. Jesus is supposed to be experienced as *the* life, whereas he had originally been experienced as the keeper of the dead. How can we resolve this nearly impossible paradox? How can our feelings get away from the death stuff? the curse? the graveyard, the endtime, the termination of the human pilgrimage?

I think it is because of these feelings that Jesus said, "God is not the God of the dead, but the God of the living."

7.
Dealing with Demons

Removing the Curse

The strongest curse word in the language is "God damn you," not "devil damn you." That the stronger feeling is God-related comes, I suppose, from primitive tradition and the Old Testament. But if we take seriously the New Testament, the curse is taken away. Jesus on the cross would have denied his entire mission if he had spoken a curse on those who crucified him. The temptation must have been almost overwhelming, but still he asked a blessing instead of a curse. While we consciously try to image God being Jesus-like, it is even easier, at the feeling level, to make God Moses-like. Jesus got the curse put on himself for trying to say God was unlike Moses—a non-judge.

To the extent we judge, we put persons down; we put the curse on them, more or less. And when we put the curse on them, we put the burden on them to justify themselves. When a person must justify himself he shows that he is under a judgment or a curse which he *works* to remove.

Now, a curse cannot be taken off by human effort simply because the assumption is that God puts the curse on and man works to get it off. Man's strength is too feeble by comparison to win in this struggle.

If I can accept the idea that God, the great power, has no will to judge, to curse, to bastardize or to kill, I do not have to defend against lesser powers doing so. At least all my resources are not used up in my defense budget. I think Jesus' ability to "cast out the demons" was his ability to take away our fear-faith regarding demons. It is in our fear that the demonic gains the strength to curse, that strength being our own human strength loaned to a nothing.

Getting Rid of Demons

Where there is no fear of death, there is no demon power. Death fear is the big fear, and the fear of demons is a lesser fear. Even the fear of demons is in many ways connected with our fear that they might destroy us; hence, death fear is at the bottom of it all. The worst part of death and demon fear is the *dread* that some power in the demon or in the stalking skeleton will be able to consume us.

In our primitive fears we are afraid that we will be *killed by death,* and the worst possible death is the one where death becomes the murdering agent. Of course we share a common fear that death has a contagion, spreading rapidly to every living thing it touches. This fear begins in early childhood where, as Sigmund Freud maintains, the child cannot imagine a death so much as he can imagine a murder: hence the child sees death as the murderer.

The power of the demonic rages in the cemetery. This was the case of the man possessed whom Jesus brought to sanity and wholeness: he lived among the tombs and he ranted, screamed and cut himself to the terror of the community around him. I think he lived among the tombs because he could not give up someone he loved who was buried in one of those tombs, and his ranting and screaming may simply have been his outpouring of grief. He disturbed the peace because there were others who heard his groans and were reminded that they, too, had some unresolved griefs.

Ancient demons are stirring again largely on a wave of combined popular fear and belief. But their very existence depends on a fear-faith to bring them into being, and where there is no belief in and fear of them they cannot hold terror for us.

The mental health of the nation has been challenged by the book *The Exorcist* by William Peter Blatty and its movie counterpart. The damage is multiplied because *The Exorcist* parades under the guise of a pseudo-psychiatric and religious respectability. All the weird happenings in the life of a young girl seem so credible when demon possession becomes the explanation for them. And of course no solution will do but exorcism.

The Splitting of Energies

We have already marked how a person puts terror into death by lending his strength to it . . . a nothing: a powerless, motionless, sterile state . . . and in lending strength to death, death gains the upper hand in the struggle. We divide the self in such a way that we invest most of its energy in an outside agent; then the energy of the self, perverted and distorted, comes back to terrify the self.

I am saying that we make death strong simply because we imagine that it has a power of its own, which it does not have. Death becomes a power, not in its own right, but in the strength loaned to it from living human imagination. In itself death is without energy or the ability to move or communicate, yet many people have not settled this truth with their feelings. They still avoid the graveyard after midnight, and they have frightful images of the "grim reaper," with the grinning skull.

Just as death gets a loan from the living in order to terrify the living, so the concept of the demonic becomes a circumstance where the energy of life (anxiety) is split and invested over against life.

A woman of thirty-one told of a phobia she had about frogs: they terrified her to the point of pure panic. She thought frogs were the ultimate source of evil and said she would rather die than have someone touch her with a frog. She imagined that frogs had a power over her. After seeing the movie *The Exorcist*, she wondered if she was possessed of a devil because of this phobia. I asked her if her problem could be solved if all frogs were destroyed. She said she didn't think it would help because there would always be the fear that there was one frog left somewhere in the world. In simple language, she needed a frog so that she could invest her self and energy in a "thing" that would overpower her, using her own strength to defeat her. Frogs have no power to destroy unless a person first gives his own strength to the frog. In this case the frog was only the instrument by which the woman fought an endless battle with herself, by which she divided herself against herself. If that instrument was removed, she would simply find another—a turtle or a lizard, or whatever.

I was unable to help this troubled woman because she could not resolve her grief over her mother, who had died four years before. She felt her own unacceptable sexuality had somehow led to the shattering and eventual death of her mother. For this feeling she couldn't forgive herself, or accept herself. She had to go on punishing herself—in the form of a cold-blooded, clammy creature that was the next thing to death. In the perversion (and hence coldness) of her own sexuality, she felt herself to be a "creep," so it was appropriate that she project her creepiness on the likes of a frog. Believing she would have to die if she were ever known was her way of saying that her death was the only acceptable sacrifice for her past. She felt she had been the cause of a death, hence she would have to pay for that death with her life.

The Demonic and the Sexual

The feelings of possession also come into play where sexual feelings and death fears get mixed together. The warm, tingling, exciting feelings of sexuality enter a child's experience very early. The prohibition of those feelings ("don't touch it lest you die") brings in another set of feelings. "To die" means cold: the original sensation brings chilling, harrowing, terrifying feelings, pretty much the opposite of the sexual or hot tingling feelings. Many people like the excitement of the cold tingling introduced by death; indeed death carries enough attraction to cause us to patronize the horror chamber at the county fair and pay our quarters for the creepy, chilling feel-

ings set off by make-believe ghosts and skeletons in
the dark. If a child thinks that he will be put to death
for his sex thoughts and wishes, he will make every
attempt to curb the normal flow of sex feeling.

In the little village where I was brought up, there
had been a marriage of first cousins. To this union
there were seven children and each of them had
some notable handicap. The community conclusion
was plain: God punished marriages that had a tinge of
incest. This was the ultimate sex taboo. The punishment of God awaited any misplaced sex feelings,
especially those that got out of "normal" channels. If
death and destruction waited on those who felt the
wrong things, then one had to declare war on all impulses that did not meet community approval.

We are reminded that in mythology and folklore
the child of incest or perversion is a monster or
demon. In primitive culture, the deformed child was
either a product of or a punishment for incest or
perversion. The movie *Rosemary's Baby* is a modern
revival of the ancient theme.

Witchcraft and voodoo are methods of controlling
life by controlling its ends: sex and death. And they
fill them both with dread and horror. The witch was
a queer, or pervert, and the ultimate expression of
cold sex (frigidity), as a popular saying reminds us:
"as cold as a witch's tit." After Macbeth's encounter
with the witches where he is promised honor and
power, Lady Macbeth takes over, saying, "Unsex me

here." She swears herself into witchiness in order to spur her husband on to claim what the witches promised; she becomes the witch to help it happen. Voodoo uses frogs and cold-blooded creatures to terrify and gain control through fear. Witchcraft and voodoo are ways of "unsexing" persons by shifting stimulation from the warmth and passion of sex to the cemetery and the chamber of horrors, or of moving sex feelings out of normal channels to the perverted channels—the creepy, the incestuous, the demonic, and the forbidden.

The Possessed

The woman with the fear of frogs felt possessed because she was at the mercy of forces beyond her control and she assumed these forces would finally do her in. She never thought of how she could win in this battle: she had to lose.

Any person may feel possessed when he is in the grip of an overpowering desire for something that will get him absolutely rejected. A sexual drive that gets focused on incest or perversion cannot be gratified without losing everything; yet to have fulfillment spells destruction, and to remain without fulfillment also means destruction.

The feeling of possession is further aggravated by guilt. A person who feels rather totally guilty allows himself to be judged and condemned by his own

imagination. Naked guilt working within him seeks
a payment or an offering to put things right again. If
a frog can make us suffer a death, as it were, we feel
we have a right to live after that death until the
guilt returns. That in turn calls for another "death,"
and the cycle goes on repeating itself from frog to
frog.

The guilt can't be cleaned up and a full payment
accepted because the whole game is unreal. At first
the person alternates between feeling absolutely
guilty and feeling that some other causes might be the
real source of trouble, but guilt leaves a person at the
mercy of all outside powers, even the whimsical hop
of a frog.

We enter a deeper dimension of the problem when
another person seeks to exploit the one whose guilt is
out of control. Just as a frog was felt to be full of
devil power, so any person can use and control the
guilty person for his own needs if he places a total
claim on the "possessed" person. In other words,
frogs don't really do anything to bind or loose the
victim; he remains pretty much self-bound. But
when a manipulating person enters the picture, we
see the ultimate in the control of one person over
another. Whether the manipulating person comes in
the name of God or the devil matters little: another
human being is bound by the power of his own fear
and guilt. He turns himself over to a person who

promises to make him suffer repeatedly, especially one who makes total claim on his freedom.

Shame and Pain

Usually the agreement necessary to bring suffering in this enslaving of the guilty offers some type of "salvation," often one of respite from the combined feelings of early childhood, of deep *pain* and *shame*. These focus on rejection, hurt, humiliation and grief, but are seldom conscious feelings. For example, a grandfather molests a five-year-old girl, creating all manner of shame and pain. A child that age seldom remembers the event, or what memory he has of it he carries in his feelings rather than in his mind. Illegitimate birth may leave deep traces of shame and pain whether or not the facts reach a child's knowledge. Birthmarks or notable deformity may inflict this same "curse." Alfred Adler went further, noting that many people have "organ inferiority" feelings: they feel deformed without actually having a deformity. From this concept, Eric Berne developed the idea of giving people the o.k. to fulfill a deep and basic need. He knew we all were looking for something to overcome the inner fears we carry over being born with some curse or stigma upon us. Such fears sometimes make us doubt our own legitimacy or, like Richard III, we wonder if we may be destined to play a monstrous and demonic role in life.

The death of a parent can be especially productive of this shame-pain feeling, and may very likely be coupled with an omnipotent feeling. One causes the death of a parent by his thoughts (and wishes); hence one had better turn one's feelings over to someone else to control: they are not safe otherwise, and they are too powerful to let loose at will.

Where the shame-pain problem revolves around sex and death, the beginning and end of life, the "child" comes through with a mixing of the "ends." Such a mixing in the feelings tends to put a layer of warmth and a layer of chill: procreation gets mixed with termination. The following combinations or "mixes" occur at the feeling level:

At the birth end	At the death end
warmth	cold
excitement	horror
thrill (with warmth)	thrill (with chill)
shame over past sex urges	cold fear over death & sex feelings
painful memory of sex	fearful dread of sex or death

Where a person has shame-pain feelings, he is usually subject to the control of the exploiter. But those who play witch, I would say, are only a small part of those who seek to control through fear-faith: many do so in politics, industry, labor, and religion, to name only a few. Wherever one person uses another against his will and judgment, a kind of witchcraft is being practiced.

Regardless of the brand of witchcraft, unnamed or of a direct, hypnotic influence through fear, the only thing that makes possible this control is the *permission* the individual grants to the controlling person or group. Guilt and fear give the handles that lead to control.

Where fear and guilt combine in pain and shame, any monstrous creature becomes possible or any nightmarish horror seems to be real. But I come back to reassert my un-faith in demonic and witchy powers. I believe that the demonic operates out of the strength we lend it as our energies get divided. Death and fear images get in the mind and tend to gain control over our feelings. But when belief in a demon is the only thing that will explain the feelings a person has, he will hold to his belief and that belief will bring many unreal things into seeming reality.

A group of little children playing around my cabin were frightened when some older children told them there were Indians out in the woods. As it began to get dark, a little six-year-old girl came to ask me about the Indians that she had already come to fear dreadfully. "Honey, don't believe those boys who are teasing you about Indians," I said, trying to put her mind at ease. "There are no Indians for you to be afraid of." But she remarked, "If there are no

Indians out there, then where did they go?" You see,
her mind had already created the Indians, so she
couldn't allow me to do away with what she had
brought into being in her fear. So it is with demons
and the phobias about frogs or whatever our minds
have built up. We bring some unreal things into a
fear-existence and we don't know how to be rid of
what we create.

Possession versus Self-Possession

I am willing to assume that there are "spirits of
evil" that are brought to being in persons. The seven
deadly sins of pride, envy, anger, sloth, avarice, glut-
tony, and lust all have a place in the human spirit.
They are to the spirit of man what cancer is to the
body; they are weeds in the wheat harvest, or ser-
pents in the fish net.

I also assume that our personal spirit is often split
into fragments as we move through life. The broken
pieces of spirit could be called demons, but I doubt
if they have any separate or independent existence.
I once asked a woman of fifty in a mental hospital to
tell me her name. At first there was no response so
several times I repeated my request: "Tell me your
name." Finally she came out with the words, "I am a
thousand," not radically different from the response
of the demoniac in the New Testament who an-

swered Jesus' question "What is your name" by saying "My name is Legion" (Mark 5:9).

It did not appear to me that this woman needed
exorcism to make her whole. Rather, her life was
being splintered from the repeated failures to be herself, not by spirits having invaded from the outside.
We examined the areas of her pain and shame. At
first she said she could only be cured by having her
head cut off. She felt so guilty that she actually
thought she would have to be sacrificed in order to
restore peace in the world around her. She thought
she was the chief cause of all trouble, and she voiced a
desire that I leave her alone. But I didn't; I repeatedly
visited her and tried to make sense out of a lot of
nonsense. The process took months, but she came to
accept herself and to accept forgiveness for all her
unacceptable feelings. She began to recognize and
visit with her two children who were faithful to
visit her and love her back to community and sanity.
The demons of shame, pain, perversion, hostility and
fear subsided, leaving her in possession of herself.
Mastered and possessed for years by these splinters of
her selfhood, they lost their power over her when
she took charge. Three years later I visited the hospital to find that she was still living with one of
her daughters.

Possession is the despairing assumption and belief
that one has to die for his own sins, the insistence on

being a proof that God is without goodness or mercy. The person who chooses this kind of thinking puts himself in competition with God and attacks goodness and truth as a wounded animal attacks his rescuer. Nevertheless, God allows him this right.

God as I image him is not a rival force with evil trying to get possession of us. Rather, I believe he is seeking to free persons for proper self-possession. We can begin to grow toward his goal for us when we turn from the habit of giving life—ours—to death, and of letting death live in us . . . when we learn to separate life from death.

Conclusion

In conclusion, let me affirm my belief that we have made death an unreal enemy and in doing so, our fears about death have cast a pallor over our lives. In not being able to let death be death, we are also unable to let life be life. Where life gets mixed with lumps of death, life loses its zest and its joy. Where we force life into stalking cadavers, not even a cemetery can be at peace.

We humans have an origin in sex and a destiny in death, and that's okay. But in our fear and panic, we tend to mix and confuse origin with destiny, beginning with ending. In other words we try to control sex impulse with death fear and we try to remove death fear with sex vitality. In the mix we tend to get our thrill and stimulation out of the chill of death and horror rather than from the warmth and creativity of life and relationship.

It is true that all life moves toward death. That is not bad. Death is a friendly part of the process; it sets a boundary against life so that we can value the days of our lives.

In our desire to be rid of death, we develop an unreal struggle from the early years. We bring religion to the rescue; then religion suffers from a deathlike taint. This association spreads over to all things holy including the "holy man," Sunday, church, prayer, the Bible and about anything else associated with God and Jesus. Religion then becomes a false fortification against death. We build a hope that our religion will help us through to a heaven that doesn't really turn us on. The gospel is emasculated in this process of promising a rescue from a black death to a pale white, bloodless eternity.

I like the great concept of Karl Olsson who affirms that the gospel is our invitation to "come to the party." We are able to be at the party and to celebrate life when we are able to give up control of our origin and our destiny, and allow that the ends of our existence are in God.

[1] Karl A. Olsson, *Come to the Party* (Waco, Texas: Word Books, 1972).

For Further Reading
From Word Books, Publisher

As Far As I Can Step by Virginia Law (QP #98016).
The intensely personal story of one woman with in-
credible insight. It will cause you to ask some searching
questions about death and will throw new light on how
muddled ideas about death prevent the emotional healing of grief.

Dialogue with Death by Abraham Schmitt (#80454).
Through his unique approach, Dr. Schmitt helps to
remove the sting from mankind's worst fear—the dread
of death. Especially helpful to ministers and personal
counselors who want to participate in the bereavement
process and help to heal the hurts of the past.   _

On the Other Side of Sorrow by Robert E. Goodrich,
Jr. (#98025). We can face sorrow bravely, knowing
that on the other side is a new strength, a new depth to
life, a new faith in God. A wonderful little book for
giving to friends. Attractive blue hardcover stamped in
gold.

Return From Tomorrow by George Ritchie, as told
to Elizabeth Sherrill (Chosen Book #76–23–6). In 1943
George Ritchie died—but lived to tell about what he saw
on the Other Side. His journey through the afterlife was
long in duration and rich in detail. The true story that
inspired Raymond Moody's bestseller, *Life After Life.*

Tracks of a Fellow Struggler by John R. Claypool (#80348, Key-Word edition #91008). For almost two decades as a pastor, John Claypool participated in the drama of suffering and death—but it was always happening to someone else. Then his own eight-year-old daughter, Laura Lee, was diagnosed as having acute leukemia. John Claypool's personal struggle will help you learn to handle grief in your own life.

We Lived with Dying by Margaret Woods Johnson (#80383). The moving story of a married couple who faced death with real interest, rather than fear. Their pilgrimage, which led to the winter day in 1964 when Wayne, a Lutheran pastor, died of cancer, is carefully and sensitively recorded. An inspiring and helpful book.

When Sorrow Comes by Robert V. Ozment (#80150). An invaluable book, prepared to ease the pain of grief for those who have lost a loved one. Words that will strengthen faith and bring comfort—from the Scriptures, poems, and from the author's own experiences and those of others.

Zest for Living by Gaines Dobbins (#80511). A documentary of the importance of zest, zeal, and enthusiasm in being successful in one's vocation and one's life. Dr. Dobbins tells you how to obtain this glorious zest—the spice of life!